# HISTORY'S
# VILLAINS

# ATTILA
## THE HUN

Scott Ingram

BLACKBIRCH®
PRESS

THOMSON
™
GALE

San Diego • Detroit • New York • San Francisco • Cleveland
New Haven, Conn. • Waterville, Maine • London • Munich

**LIBRARY OF CONGRESS CATALOGING-IN-PUBLICATION DATA**

Ingram, Scott (William Scott)
  Attila the Hun / by W. Scott Ingram.
    p. cm. — (History's greatest villains)
  Includes bibliographical references and index.
  Summary: Discusses the Roman Empire, its collapse at the hands of barbarian hordes led
  by Attila the Hun, and Attila's legacy.
   ISBN 1-56711-628-0 (alk. paper)
   1. Attila, d. 453—Juvenile literature. 2. Huns—Biography-Juvenile literature. 3. Huns—
  History—Juvenile literature. [1. Attila, d. 453. 2. Kings, queens, rulers, etc. 3. Huns—
  History.] I. Title. II. Series.
  D141 .I54 2003
  936—dc21                                                                    2002003378

**Printed in United States**
10 9 8 7 6 5 4 3 2 1

# CONTENTS

# Introduction:
## "I Shall Hurl
## the First Spear"

In June of 451, two huge armies faced each other across the wide, flat plains near Châlons, a city located in what is today western France. One army was made up of fighters from non-European tribes, who faced soldiers of the Roman army. Like the Roman Empire itself, however, the Roman army had grown weak over the preceding century.

For centuries, the Roman army—divided into units called legions—had been the most powerful fighting force in the world. Their military might gave Roman emperors absolute control over more than 40 million people from the British Isles to the Middle East. Unimaginable wealth—gold, spices, cloth, and other riches—had poured into the Roman treasury, sent as taxes, tribute, and peace offerings from every corner of the empire.

Slowly, though, drought, disease, and internal struggles for power had weakened Rome. Outside its

4

borders, peoples from the distant lands to the north and the endless plains of central Asia had attacked the edges of the empire.

By 400, warlike groups had begun to carve up the Roman Empire into smaller kingdoms. Some took over lands once governed by Rome and established their own states. Other groups formed alliances with Roman leaders. The troops from those alliances were gathered outside Châlons alongside the Roman soldiers. They had joined forces to battle a fierce army and a feared leader who had conquered much of central and eastern Europe.

The attackers were the Huns, people originally from Asia. They were led by a man known throughout the empire as the "Scourge [punishment] of God." He was the king of the Huns—Attila. A historian of the time described Attila as "short of stature, with a broad chest and a large head. His eyes were small, his beard thin and sprinkled with gray... and he had a flat nose and a swarthy complexion."

By 451, Attila and his Hun army had killed thousands of people, destroyed hundreds of cities, and spread terror across much of Europe. In cities he conquered, he had ordered the roads lined with the heads of defeated enemies. Prisoners were thrown under

*The Battle of Châlons was fought by more than 250,000 soldiers.*

huge Hun war wagons and crushed. The people of Europe feared no man more than Attila the Hun.

Now, as Attila's 100,000-man army prepared for battle, the king of the Huns sat on his horse and spoke

ATTILA THE HUN

to his troops. Attila was said to love war so much that his eyes rolled back in his head from sheer pleasure during battle, and his huge army listened to him with great respect. The Hun leader spoke in his usual fierce manner before the Battle of Châlons: "Seek swift victory. Show your cunning, Huns. Revel in the slaughter of the enemy." Finally, Attila challenged his men as he had over the past eight years. He said, "I shall hurl the first spear at the foe. If any man stand at rest while Attila fights, he is a dead man."

With that, the "Scourge of God" rode to meet the enemy. Soon, a conflict so fierce took place that legends claimed the ghosts of the dead continued to fight after the battle was over. And today, more than 1,500 years later, the name Attila remains a symbol of terror and brutality.

## CHAPTER 1

# THE PEOPLE OF THE STEPPES

Today, the name "Attila the Hun" creates an image of a villain who destroyed and terrorized defenseless people in the early European world. He is widely considered one of the fiercest conquerors in history. Yet, despite the fear linked with his name, Attila was sole ruler of the Huns for only eight years. He came to power at a time when Rome, one of the mightiest empires ever known, was in the final years of its existence.

*Opposite: The Huns were fierce nomads who swept into Europe from Asia.*

It is possible that if Attila had not come to power when he did, he might not have made the mark on history that he has. His rise to power was the result of the movement of his people, the Huns. For several centuries before Attila's birth, the Huns had moved steadily—and brutally—across Asia to the edge of Europe. They arrived in Europe at a time when the mighty Roman Empire was near collapse.

## Tribal Migrations

By the late 300s, non-Roman groups had established territories in areas of southern Europe and North Africa once ruled by Rome. Those people had moved from their original homelands because those homelands had come under attack by the Huns. For several decades during the fourth and fifth centuries, the Huns were the most feared of all tribes.

For centuries, the Huns and other non-Roman groups were known as "barbarians." The term generally referred to people whose homeland was outside the borders of the Roman Empire and who did not speak Latin or Greek, the most widely spoken languages in Europe at that time. The word "barbarian" originally came from the Greek language and meant "foreigner" or "stranger." To the Greeks, the languages of the people from northern Europe had a harsh tone that sounded like "bar-bar-bar." Thus, "bar-bar-ian" became the label given to them. Only in later years did the word become a synonym for uncivilized warriors.

Because the Huns did not have a written language, little is known of their origins or of their culture before they arrived in Europe. Historians in ancient China during the second century B.C. wrote about fierce attacks by people from a region north of China, known today as Mongolia. The Chinese referred to these invaders as the Hsiung-nu. Most historians agree that the Hsiung-nu were the same nomads who came to be known in Europe as the Huns.

These invaders from central Asia were feared for their exceptional ability to fight from horseback. The Hsiung-nu were so ferocious that for protection from them, the Chinese built an enormous stone and earth wall—30 feet high and more than 1,500 miles long—across their northern border. Large portions of this fortification still stand today. Known as the Great Wall of China, it is one of the wonders of the ancient world.

When the Huns found the path into China blocked, they turned west. By about 200, they had begun to move across Asia toward eastern Europe. As they moved, the Huns forced native people off their lands.

The Great Wall of China was built to keep out the Hsiung-nu, forerunners of the Huns.

ATTILA THE HUN

As these people fled, they warned any groups they encountered about the strange-looking warriors that seemed to be half-horse and half-human.

## Nomads and Warriors

The Huns did not face any geographic obstacles, such as mountains or oceans, that halted their westward movement. Instead, there were only the endless, flat plains known as the steppes—grasslands that extended from northern China to the Danube River in eastern Europe.

It is unknown whether a drought or other natural disaster made the Huns migrate west rather than establish a kingdom on the steppes. It is known that during the first centuries of the Christian era, average temperatures fell in northern Europe. Historical weather records have

13

# THE BARBARIAN CONQUESTS

By the end of the fourth century, the Roman Empire was crumbling. The first large military invasion by a German tribe into Roman territory took place in 376 A.D. This tribe was known as the Visigoths.

The Visigoths had settled in Pannonia, today the countries of Hungary and Romania. In the 370s, they were forced off their land by the Hunnish migration. In turn, the Visigoths invaded the eastern region of the Roman Empire, crossed the Danube River, and fought a large Roman force at the Battle of Adrianople in 378. The Visigoth cavalry crushed the Roman army, and killed more than 40,000 soldiers.

The defeat signaled the end of Roman military power—and was the first example in Roman history of the superiority of mounted warriors to foot soldiers. Adrianople was the worst defeat the Romans had suffered in more than three centuries. One Roman historian called the battle, "the end of all humanity, the end of the world."

After their tremendous victory, the Visigoths settled first in the northern region of modern-day Italy. In 400, under King Alaric, they began to conquer the region, and finally sacked and destroyed Rome in 410. Over the next 50 years, they moved across France and eventually established a kingdom in Spain and southern France.

Soon other barbarian tribes began to cross the Danube and Rhine Rivers, and take control of lands that once belonged to the dying empire. The Franks moved across the Rhine and into modern-day northern France, where they established an empire. The Vandals fought south through France and Spain. They crossed the Mediterranean at the Strait of Gibraltar, then took control of the Roman territory in North Africa. Everywhere they migrated, the Vandals—whose name in their language meant "the brave ones"—left behind ruins that gave their name its modern meaning.

Elsewhere, barbarian tribes such as the Angles and the Saxons crossed the

English Channel and drove out the Romans stationed in Britain. The Ostrogoths established a large kingdom near Rome. The fiercest of all the German tribes, the Lombards, took control of northern Italy. Throughout the empire, barbarians brought destruction and death to Romans. Of those times, a Roman poet wrote, "In village, villa, field…down every roadway and at every turning, grief, destruction, and arson are revealed. Why tell the deathroll brought by endless fear? Why count how many unto death are hurled when you see your own day hurrying near?"

*The Germanic tribes from north of the Rhine River attacked the borders of the Roman Empire.*

also shown that decades of lower temperatures in northern Europe led to periods of drought in eastern Europe.

It may have been such a period of drought that kept the Huns on the move in search of grazing areas for their livestock. Slowly at first, then in waves, thousands of these nomads migrated across the steppes with their herds of cattle, sheep, and, especially, horses.

The Huns' small horses—about the size of large ponies, with thick legs and a sturdy build—were their most prized possessions. A Roman veterinarian described the Huns' horses as having "large heads... protruding eyes... strong necks. Their manes hang down to their knees... and their tails [are] shaggy.... Their stature is long rather than tall."

So important were horses that they were religious objects in early Hun culture. White horses were sacrificed, and Hun warriors drank the animals' blood. Many people who encountered the Huns came to believe that the nomads were part of their horses, or that they lived on them. In truth, the Huns were known to eat, sleep, and hold meetings with visitors while on horseback.

As they moved across the steppes, the Huns set up their horsehair tents, called "yurts," on wheeled wooden platforms. Teams of oxen pulled these early mobile homes across the endless river of grass.

*Even in modern times, the people of the Mongolian plains depend on horses for transportation and yurts for shelter.*

The Huns developed a nomadic lifestyle to survive in the Mongolian plains—the eastern edge of the steppes— where their culture originated. The Eurasian steppes are a huge region that spans two continents. The harsh

17

# Two Capitals

By the fourth century, the Roman Empire had been in decline for 200 years. In addition to the economic stress, another important reason for the weakening of the empire was the spread of a new religious faith—Christianity.

Rome's execution of Jesus Christ in the distant province of Judea in the Middle East in about 33, gave rise to a religious movement that did not worship the emperor as most Roman subjects had. Instead these people became followers of Jesus Christ—Christians. They were devoted to the worship of one god rather than many Roman gods, and they did not regard the emperor as divine. The new faith began to break away from the Roman culture and traditions that had been established over a wide area.

Despite brutal treatment by Roman rulers, Christians carried their new faith to every corner of the empire. Finally, in 312, a civil war broke out between two Roman leaders who claimed the title of emperor. Before a key battle, one leader, Constantine, claimed that he saw a flaming cross—a symbol of Christianity—in the sky. After he won the battle, and control of the empire, Constantine proclaimed that from that day on, Christians would be allowed to practice their religion.

Constantine became the first Christian emperor of the Roman Empire. At that time, the capital of the empire was not Rome. That once great city had fallen into decay. Rather than rebuild Rome,

Constantine built a new capital city, far from Rome, in the country today known as Turkey. That city, called Constantinople, is now the city of Istanbul. It was built on a peninsula between the Black Sea and the Mediterranean Sea.

After the construction of Constantinople, the Roman Empire became a kingdom with two capitals. Ravenna was the capital of the Western Roman Empire, and Constantinople was the capital of the Eastern Roman Empire.

*Emperor Constantine converted to Christianity after an important military victory.*

climate made the development of an agriculture-based civilization impossible. The only plants that grow there—grasses and shrubs—are inedible for humans. Thus, nomad societies developed around the domestication of grazing animals such as sheep, horses, and cattle.

Once livestock herds had eaten all the plants in one area, the tribe migrated to another area. In many cases, they encountered other groups who were also nomads and had come to the areas for the same reason. The competition for grazing lands meant that the Huns had to drive out anyone else on the lands they entered; therefore, aggression was a normal feature of the society.

A life of constant travel meant that every Hun child learned to ride a horse as soon as he or she could walk. The result was an army that was essentially one huge cavalry force. Hun warriors often traveled with a string of several horses so that they would always have a fresh, well-rested horse for any attack.

The Huns' outstanding ability to fight from horseback was due to an important piece of equipment they developed—the stirrup. This foot piece allowed the Hun warriors to remain securely on their horses with both hands free to fight. In a spear attack, this meant that a Hun who struck his foe would transfer the weight of both the horse and the rider through the spear as it struck a foe. This increased power of the thrust allowed Huns to penetrate the armor worn by their enemies.

The spear, however, was not the main weapon of the Huns. Their most important weapon was the bow and arrow. The curved Hunnish bows were flexible enough to allow fighters to draw their bowstrings back a foot or more. This enabled them to shoot arrows that usually traveled more than 1,000 feet (300 meters) and killed an enemy at half that distance.

One other fact led to the terror that the Huns caused as they approached the outer regions of Europe. They were much larger than average people of that time. Their nomadic lifestyle was built around a diet of milk and meat—a high-protein diet, which contributes to height in humans. In ancient times, the Huns seemed like giants—especially when they were on horseback.

Those who fled from these nomadic warriors told terrifying stories of huge, fur-clad, tattooed fighters. The fast-moving troops covered enormous distances, and sometimes changed horses several times a day to advance into new lands. By the fourth century, the Huns had crossed Asia and entered Europe. They moved west around the Caspian Sea to the Black Sea, then south toward the Danube River, which served as the eastern border of the Roman Empire.

# THE HUNNISH BOW

The Huns' bow was a combination (called a composite) weapon made of wood, bone, and animal sinews. The sections of the bow were held together by glue made from fish bladders and wrapped with tree bark. The most advanced weapon of its time, it was bent into a deep curve to make it easier to handle on horseback. The reverse-curved "ears" on each end of the bow made the weapon's snapping action very powerful. Its shorter length allowed it to clear the horse's body as the riders attacked at full gallop. Thus Hun warriors could shoot forward, backward, and to the sides with deadly accuracy.

The Huns' arrows were made of wood with bone inlays for added strength. Each warrior went into battle with thirty arrows. This supply did not last long, so a traveling arrow work-man—a fletcher—accompanied each unit, and re-supplied warriors as quickly as they ran out.

The bow's usefulness in battle was increased by the Huns' horsemanship and by their unusual fighting tactics. At the height of a Hun attack, for example, the Huns might turn their horses and pretend to retreat. When soldiers pursued them, the Huns turned around and shot the enemy as they rode in the opposite direction.

## The Huns Face the Romans

Rome had ruled much of Europe and the Middle East for almost 400 years. At the height of its power, in about 120, the Roman Empire stretched from the country known today as Great Britain across all of Europe south of the Rhine River as far as the Danube River. Roman rule also extended to the northern coast of Africa from the Strait of Gibraltar to the Nile River and north to Syria. If it were in existence today, the Roman Empire would be the fourth largest country in the world.

By the time the Huns approached the Danube in the fourth century, however, the empire had been in decline for 200 years. It had grown too large to manage efficiently. In addition, the spread of a new religion known as Christianity had led to civil wars. These wars pitted the followers of the new faith against those who continued to follow the traditions of worshiping gods and absolute obedience to the emperor, who was considered divine. The internal strife weakened the empire and made it an inviting target to the invaders from the steppes.

The invading Huns faced a Roman army that vastly outnumbered them. Yet, even with greater numbers of soldiers and sturdier iron weapons, the Roman troops

By the beginning of the fifth century, many of the great cities of the Roman Empire had fallen to invaders.

on the edges of the weakened empire were no match for the Huns on horseback. Not only were the Hun riders more agile because of the stirrup, the Hunnish bow was a much more effective weapon than the longbow used by Roman archers.

The most widely used battle technique of the time—fighting in orderly columns at close quarters—did not work against the Huns, who rode effortlessly, and fired arrows from all directions—sometimes even while pretending to retreat. A Roman military historian wrote this description of Huns in battle—"When attacked they will sometimes engage in regular battle . . . filling the air with discordant cries. More often, however, they fight in no regular order of battle, but by extremely swift and sudden movements, they disperse, and then rapidly come together again in loose array . . . they pillage the camp of their enemy almost before he has become aware of their approach. They are the most terrible of warriors because they fight at a distance with missile weapons [arrows] having sharpened bones fastened to the shaft. When in close combat, they fight without regard to their safety, and while their enemy is intent on parrying the thrust of swords, they throw a net over him and so entangle his limbs that he loses all power."

**The Roman Empire**
**116 A.D.**
The empire at its greatest extent
at the time of Emperor Trajan

In addition to their unusual fighting style, Hun warriors displayed a level of brutality that shocked the people of the time. They were known to cut the scalps off their conquered enemies and wear them on their belts. They sometimes tortured captives to death by peeling the skin slowly from their bodies, as one might skin an animal. Tales were told of Huns who conquered a fortress, then made the captives lie on the floor. The Huns laid heavy wooden boards over them and set up heavy tables and chairs on the boards. The warriors then drank and ate at the tables while their weight slowly crushed the screaming captives beneath the boards.

Ammianus Marcellinus, a Roman historian in the third century A.D., wrote: "The nation of Huns . . . surpasses all other barbarians in the wildness of life. And though they do bear the likeness of men (of a very ugly pattern), they are so little advanced in civilization that they make no use of fire, nor any kind of relish, in the preparation of their food, but feed upon the roots they find in the field and the half-raw flesh of any sort of animal. I say half-raw because they give it a kind of cooking by placing it between their own thighs and the backs of their horses."

As the Huns continued their conquest across Asia and Europe, they arrived in a region of flat plains the

The Huns were feared for their lightning-fast attacks and their brutal treatment of captives.

Romans called Pannonia. This large, grassy flatland provided grazing areas for their livestock, and the Huns established settlements there at the eastern side of the Danube River. (Today, much of this region is known as the country of Hungary.)

Remaining settled in one region, however, presented a challenge for the nomadic Huns. As nomads, they had never developed a merchant class or an economy based on agricultural production. War, therefore, became the only way they had to acquire wealth, and tributes—payment for protection—from conquered peoples became the main money supply of the Hun treasury. Leaders who paid for peace became the foundation of the Huns' economy as they established a Hunnish Kingdom.

In the late fourth century, under the rule of a king named Uldin, the Huns defeated a large Roman force in several battles around the Danube River. They also added to their reputation for

# THE HORSE AND THE HUNS

Horsemanship played a huge role in the Huns' military success. By the time of Attila, Huns, and other people from central Asia, had fought on horseback for almost 1,000 years. It was a tradition that gave the Huns an enormous battlefield edge over the foot soldiers of Rome or barbarian tribes during the early years of their conquest in Europe.

The prehistoric ancestor of the horse, eohippus, was a three-toed, fox-sized animal that first evolved in North America. Millions of years later, a large, hooved, horselike animal migrated across the land bridge that connected Asia and North America. Horses then vanished from the Americas until Spanish conquistadors brought them over on ships during their conquests of the Native American peoples in Central and South America in the 16th century.

Archeologists agree that the earliest humans hunted horses for food. Recent evidence indicates that the horse was first domesticated about 5,000 years ago, long after other livestock and companion animals. By that time, humans and dogs had been companions for 9,000 years. People in various regions of the world had herded goats, sheep, and cattle for nearly 5,000 years before the horse became domesticated.

It took a long time for horses to become domesticated because it was difficult to capture and tame them. Cattle and sheep were slower than horses, more docile, and easier to herd. Horses were not only fast, they resisted the bit and bridle, and were wary of humans.

Evidence of horse domestication has been discovered by archeologists in the steppes of central Asia, central

Russia, and the country known today as Kazakhstan. There, horse skulls have been uncovered with teeth worn down by bits.

Scientists who have studied unearthed horse skeletons believe the first domesticated horses were about the size of large ponies, about 14 hands (56") at the shoulder. At first, horses were treated like other livestock. Mares supplied milk. Horse flesh provided food, hides were used to make tents or clothes, and manure could be dried to make fuel for fires.

Over the centuries, Asian tribes realized they could become more mobile by using the tamest horses to pull carts that transported household belongings. Thus, the first use of the horse was as a beast of burden. After nomads had used horses to pull heavy loads, it was a natural next step to ride them while herding.

An athletic man or woman could have ridden a pony-sized horse without a saddle, but some control other than simply grabbing the animal's mane was needed. Originally, this may have been a rope around the jaw or some sort of bridle. Antler cheekpieces, held in place by soft mouthpieces of rope, rawhide, or sinew, have been uncovered at sites north of the Black Sea in the steppes.

Mounted soldiers first appeared in historical records around 1,000 B.C. They were warriors from central Asia and were skilled at shooting the bow and arrow as they rode. These warriors became part of the forces that made the ancient Persian Empire—in the modern Middle Eastern countries of Iraq and Iran—one of the most successful in ancient times before the rise of Rome.

Although horses were used in the armies of the Greek and Roman Empires, they generally pulled supply wagons or chariots used by commanders. In most cases, cavalry troops rode to a battle site, then dismounted to fight.

The rise of the Huns to power was largely accomplished because of the speed of their cavalry units. With horses that could outrun the fastest enemy scout, the first warning many villages had of a Hun attack was a thunder of hooves and a cloud of arrows raining down upon them.

savagery when they cut off the heads of the military officers and sent them to the Roman governors. The ease with which they had defeated the once-mighty Romans encouraged the Huns to cross the Danube and venture further west and south into Europe.

By 400, the Huns controlled a region from the Caspian Sea to the Danube—an area of land nearly as large as that of Rome at its height of power. From Pannonia, King Ruga, the ruler who succeeded Uldin, began to launch attacks across eastern Europe. Hun forces raided countless settlements; they captured gold and slaves, and kidnapped wealthy civilians. The spoils of battle were taken to the Huns' main settlement, Szeged, which was located on a tributary of the Danube River.

Ruga's older brother, a warrior named Mundzuk, was a powerful second-in-command of the Hun forces. In the early fifth century, Mundzuk's wife gave birth to a son, Bleda. In 406, Mundzuk's second son, Attila, was born. The two boys grew up as Hun royalty while the Huns' empire expanded.

Among Ruga's most feared cavalry was a unit known as the Tarkan warriors, who began the custom of taking wealthy people as hostages and bringing them back to Szeged to be held for ransom. One hostage was a young

Roman boy named Aetius. Because he was the son of a noble, Aetius was not treated as a common prisoner. Instead, he and young Attila became friends. During Aetius's time as a hostage, which lasted more than a year, the young Roman rode and hunted with Attila. Aetius even learned to speak the Huns' language before his ransom was paid and he returned to his family.

## CHAPTER 2

# THE RISE OF ATTILA

In the first decades of the fifth century, while Bleda and Attila learned horsemanship and other arts of war, Ruga and Mundzuk continued to attack settlements. In 422, Ruga attacked Roman towns along the lower Danube River near the Black Sea. After Theodosius II, the emperor of the Eastern Roman Empire, lost several battles to the Huns, he offered to pay an annual tribute of 350 pounds of gold. In return, Ruga and his force agreed to leave the Romans in peace.

In the last years of Ruga's reign, another method to raise money was developed. Several areas along the northern border of the Roman

Empire were under attack from Germanic barbarians. Roman troops were undermanned and needed the help of well-trained fighting forces. Ruga allowed some of his men to fight in distant lands for the Roman military in return for payment. The middleman in this arrangement between the Romans and the Huns was Aetius, who had risen to the rank of Roman general while still in his twenties.

In return for allowing his Hun cavalry to fight for the Romans, Ruga received gold to add to the tribute money already in the Hunnish treasury. In addition, the Romans gave the Huns rights to the land of Pannonia. For the first time, the Huns had a permanent homeland.

*Attila (above) and his brother Bleda grew up as Hun royalty.*

## The Rule of Brothers

In 433, Ruga died and, because Mundzuk had died several years before, Bleda became the new king of the Huns. Attila was given command of forces in an area south of the main Hun homeland, near the mouth of the Danube River in what is today the country of Romania.

After Ruga's death, the Roman government in Constantinople ignored the tribute agreements between the Huns and Theodosius II. Bleda and Attila believed that the agreements should still be followed. They demanded a meeting with Theodosius's representatives in a town called Margus, in the modern country of Serbia. Their failure to meet, the brothers warned the Romans, would result in an attack by the Hun forces on the Roman settlements.

Bleda and Attila arrived on the outskirts of Margus to wait for the arrival of the Roman ambassadors. They pitched their tents in plain view of city walls, but insisted that all talks be held on horseback. Although the Hun leaders could easily have negotiated in their large, comfortable tents, to deal from horseback reminded the Romans that Hun horsemen could unleash devastation and terror to the region if an agreement was not reached.

The sight of the fierce young Hun kings on horseback was convincing. Theodosius's representatives doubled their yearly tribute from 350 to 700 pounds of gold. In addition, they agreed not to enter into any alliances with peoples who were enemies of the Huns.

The Treaty of Margus was a great success for Bleda and Attila. For the first time, Hun leaders were able to set the terms of an agreement without sending forces into battle. They achieved benefits for their economy and security for their homeland without the loss of a single man.

This agreement, however, did not mean the Huns had given up their warlike ways or their dreams of further conquest. Bleda and Attila turned their men toward western Europe. Soon, the Huns battled other groups that had settled along the banks of the Rhine River in northern Europe.

By 440, the Huns—mainly under the command of Bleda—had gained control of enormous areas in the region between Rome and Constantinople. The Romans were again forced to raise the amount of gold they paid yearly to the Huns.

In 444, Bleda died under mysterious circumstances. Most historians believe that Attila became dissatisfied with serving under his older brother and had Bleda murdered. This theory is supported by records of arguments between the brothers during the years in which they shared power. In 445, Attila was recognized as the king of the Huns. He took control of an empire, and a culture, which had changed from the Huns' original traditions.

## The Kingdom of Attila

The image of Attila that has come down through the centuries is that of a primitive, bloodthirsty ruler. Although it is true that he was among the most brutal men of his era, Attila was also a king who sought to expand and enrich his kingdom through alliances and trade rather than constant warfare. His goal was to build an empire equal to that of the Romans at the height of their power.

Attila's desire to change arose mainly because he became the leader of the Huns at a time when they had ceased their nomadic lifestyle. He, in fact, had known little of the wandering ways of his ancestors. He grew up in a Hunnish homeland in the eastern region of modern-day Hungary, in a capital that had been established at Szeged.

Despite this way of life, Attila believed that, because of the Huns' history and reputation, he was considered less than equal to other powerful rulers—more of a killer than a king. Part of this perception of him may also have been because of his Asian race and his non-Christian religious background.

*The attacks of the Huns' cavalry overwhelmed opponents.*

Whatever the reason, Attila believed that in order to maintain power, he had to use methods in addition to war. This meant establishing trade relations for economic growth. It also meant that the Huns needed to develop agricultural techniques for food production. Like the Romans before him, to expand his borders and create an empire beyond Pannonia, Attila had to bring people of other races and cultures willingly under Hunnish control and protection.

To reach these goals, Attila sought the advice of people who were more educated in areas of diplomacy and economics than most Huns. In the first years of his reign, Attila's circle of advisers began to include a large number of foreigners. His closest military advisor was a Roman named Orestes, whose son became the last emperor of the Western Roman Empire. One economic advisor came from modern-day Italy. Another came from what is today France. Two were from Greece. Attila needed the help of these men because they spoke and wrote the main languages of the time, Latin and Greek. The Huns, with no written language, faced difficulties in drawing up treaties and other agreements.

Although Attila brought many outsiders into his circle of advisers, in no way did he change his warlike nature. While his advisers helped maintain territory

# ATTILA'S WIVES

The culture over which Attila ruled was polygamous—rulers and men of wealth had several wives. Most privileges and inheritance were passed from the father to the children of his first wife. Attila was believed to have had as many as eighteen wives, with whom he had more than fifty children. His first wife, named Kreka, gave birth to three sons.

The youngest of the three, Ernak, became his father's favorite.

Not all of Attila's wives happily accepted the arrangement. One famous story passed down through the centuries tells of Attila being served what he thought was the meat of a young animal. He later learned that one of his unhappy wives had served him a meal of two of his sons!

under control, Attila continued his quest for more land and people to conquer.

Attila's ability to bring such people into his court was an indication to rulers of his time that so-called barbarians led relatively comfortable lives. Priscus, a Greek historian, lived among the Huns for many weeks in 449, and interviewed Romans who served Attila. One Roman adviser described to Priscus the appeal of living with the Huns: "It is the wholesome life a man has the right to expect, secure from injustice, free from insults from the powerful, the burden of taxation, the corruption of the court."

The few historical fragments of Priscus's work that have survived over the centuries show that, during Attila's time, Hun nobles wore gold and silver jewelry, Indian pearls, and silks. They ate dates and spiced their food with pepper. Many of these luxuries were paid to the Huns in tribute. Others were acquired by trading the most valuable commodities in the Huns' world—their horses.

By the time Attila took power, many Hun dwellings in Pannonia were wooden houses rather than horsehair tents. Attila's own palace was built of wood, with rooms divided by silk tapestries. Baths of marble and stone were built in the palace and in the homes of other wealthy or powerful members of the Hun community.

## A Changing Military Force

Changes in Hunnish society that came about during Attila's life also led to changes in the Huns' style of warfare. In 445, the Huns were still a feared and warlike people whose main attack force remained a quick-striking

*As Attila's power grew, his army consisted of more foot soldiers than cavalry.*

cavalry. As their territorial rule expanded, the Huns encountered walled cities and other large fortresses against which the cavalry was not effective. By that point, the Huns had conquered a large number of groups and forced their defeated foes to enlist in an infantry. Thus, a large Hunnish army of foot soldiers could surround a town or fortress and lay siege to it. Should an enemy force emerge from an enclosure, the cavalry was poised to strike it down.

The transition from an entirely mounted force to a combination force also took place because the Huns' conquests had brought them to an environment that no longer supported the type of military culture in which they had evolved. When the Huns were nomads on the vast steppes, they had unlimited grazing areas for their horses. Once they settled in Pannonia, however, their grazing area became much smaller, and they could not sustain a large horse population. Thus the size of their mounted fighting units became limited. The Huns solved this problem by establishing a force of foot soldiers from conquered groups. In this way, the Hun army—now an army of mixed tribes—became a fighting force as large as any in the ancient world.

When Huns invaded new regions, many people fled from the area, but those who remained and were unable

# What Became of the Gold?

During the fifth century, gold played an important role in the economy and in the art of Hun society. Huge amounts of gold—thousands of pounds a year—came to the Hun treasury as tribute from the Romans and other kingdoms. Much of the gold was used to make jewelry, drinking goblets, knives, horse harnesses, and countless other objects. The Huns also followed the practice of burying valuables with a wealthy person who died. Attila is believed to be buried with a fortune in golden objects in his coffin.

*A gold ring among the Huns' treasure was made in Greece.*

After the Hun Empire fell from power, the golden treasures were slowly forgotten over the centuries. Then, in the early twentieth century, a peasant woman appeared at the Szeged Museum and showed the director a piece of gold jewelry that she had found on her farm outside the city. The director recognized the piece as Hun jewelry and formed an expedition to search for more of the Hun treasure.

Although the expedition members found dozens of gold objects in the region, scientists believed there had to be much more gold. Further investigation revealed that, for generations, poor farmers in the area had uncovered Hun burial areas and used the gold for money and trade. The gold that was taken to the Szeged Museum, where it remains on display today, represented only a tiny fraction of the amount that once filled the Hun treasury.

to serve in the military were allowed to continue to raise crops and livestock as they had always done. In this way, the Huns were able to secure food and use the extra crops for peaceful agricultural trade. The people known as the Gepids were the most productive of any group under Hun control. Gepid farms grew wheat, barley, peas, and fruit. The juice from the cherries grown by the Gepids was a favorite drink of the Huns, and mutton from sheep raised among the Gepids was the most commonly eaten meat.

## CHAPTER 3

# ATTILA'S FIRST CONQUESTS

Although Attila took control of the Huns at a time when they had a settled homeland, he was not satisfied with the extent of his kingdom. Thus, his first goal as king was to conquer the lands closest to his own borders. These were the lands and cities under the control of a governor he knew well: Theodosius II.

In 447, Attila began his first military campaign. He headed south from Szeged along the Balkan Peninsula toward Greece, where he planned to conquer large cities and eventually to overrun the capital of Constantinople.

Attila's force included Hun cavalry units, but was mainly made up of foot soldiers from other barbarian tribes. Because his army was on foot rather than horseback, it moved more slowly than Hun cavalry of the past. It also brought greater destruction and death in cities that fell to Attila, because its raids were not hit-and-run attacks. Instead they were invasions intended to utterly destroy and depopulate cities to prevent them from being rebuilt.

Historical records show that Attila destroyed more than seventy cities as his force moved south. With each

*Theodosius II ruled Constantinople for the first half of the fifth century.*

conquest, his reputation for brutality grew. Enemy soldiers were beheaded by Attila's men, and their heads

ATTILA THE HUN

displayed along roadsides. Homes were burned and anything of value was taken.

Callinicus, a Roman Christian, witnessed some of the devastation. He wrote that when the Huns conquered, "There were so many murders and bloodletting that the dead could not be numbered . . . they took captive the churches and monasteries and slew (killed) the monks and maidens in great quantities."

The brutality of the Huns was more than simply a bloodthirsty frenzy. It was calculated to create so much terror that by the time the Huns came close to the enormous city of Constantinople—which they could not conquer by attack—the people within its walls might surrender without a fight. Attila concentrated his killing among the military, the nobility, and the clergy. The military and nobility were obvious targets for any conquering foes. The clergy was killed because Attila knew how Christianity had turned people away from obedience to Roman emperors, and he feared similar effects among the people in his own expanding empire.

As planned, the news of the destruction brought by Attila and the Huns quickly reached Constantinople. Soon, the people of the city were in a panic. They knew that if the capital fell to the Hun ruler, the entire Eastern Roman Empire would be under Attila's control.

*The walls built by the people of Constantinople to keep out the Huns still stand today and are known as the Walls of Theodosius.*

As the invaders marched closer, citizens fled from Constantinople. Even the emperor, Theodosius II, prepared to leave the city. Fortunately for the city and its citizens, Attila's army encountered two obstacles along the way. The first occurred when a Roman military leader, Arneglicus, bravely led his troops out to attack Attila rather than wait for him to reach the city. The Roman troops fought fiercely, and although Arneglicus was killed, the fight delayed the Huns long enough to give the people who remained in Constantinople time to strengthen the city walls and build defensive towers.

Despite the delay, Attila continued his march toward Constantinople. Soon, however, the army was completely stopped by a second, deadly obstacle: disease. Malaria, a disease caused by mosquitoes, and dysentery, a disease caused by drinking unclean water, hit the troops. Thousands of Hun soldiers died, and thousands more were left too weak to fight. By the time Attila had enough healthy men, most of the people who had fled the city had returned. Now that Constantinople had stronger defenses and a larger population to defend their homes, Attila felt that his army was not strong enough to conquer the city, especially now that it was fortified by walls more than 30 feet high.

## A Murder Plot

After he made the decision not to attack, Attila withdrew from the area around Constantinople. Still, the devastation caused by his campaign remained a fresh memory. Many people within the borders of the Eastern Roman Empire—and in Constantinople itself—feared another Hun invasion once Attila added healthy soldiers to his ranks.

Although he knew it would take months to rebuild the size of his force, Attila believed that his mere presence in the vicinity of a Roman city such as Constantinople was a powerful threat, and he was right. He boldly sent several of his closest advisers to the court of Theodosius to demand higher payments of gold—even as his army was moved away. Theodosius, who had known Hun pressure for most of his rule, once again increased the tribute he paid to Attila, even though it meant he had to raise the taxes on his people.

Attila soon decided that several thousand pounds of gold a year was not enough. He wanted the rights to a large area of territory still under Roman control. As he and his brother had done with the Treaty of Margus, Attila wanted to gain land without risking the lives of his men. The Hun king sent one of his closest advisers, Edika, to Theodosius with his demand for Roman land.

Inside the emperor's palace in the spectacular capital, Edika was greeted by an adviser to the emperor named Bigilas, who spoke the Huns' language. Bigilas took Edika to meet Theodosius and his advisers. Edika offered greetings from Attila to the emperor and praised the beauty of the palace.

Bigilas noticed the way that Edika admired the surroundings and asked the Hun if he would like to live a life of such comfort and wealth. It would be a simple matter, others in the room said. All Edika had to do was to assassinate Attila. To their surprise, Edika seemed interested in their proposal. Then they asked how much gold it would take to persuade Edika to murder the Hun king. Fifty pounds to buy the silence of my guards, he answered, and the promise of an easy life once the killing was carried out.

Soon an assassination plan had been worked out with the approval of Theodosius. Edika was to return to Attila's camp, and a party of Romans would follow. Only Edika and Bigilas would know of the plan. The others would believe that they were going to settle a treaty agreement with Attila. Bigilas would secretly carry the gold to pay Edika's men. Once Attila was dead, Edika would return to Constantinople with the Romans.

The leader of the group, who knew nothing of the plan, was a Roman politician named Maximinus. He believed that he was on a mission to the Huns' camp to establish diplomatic relations. Maximinus invited his friend, the historian Priscus, to travel with the party. Priscus's description of the journey and the events that followed is the only eyewitness record of Attila during the early years of his rule.

In 449, the Roman party set out from Constantinople to meet Attila. The group made its way across territory that had been conquered by the Huns two years before. Once they reached the Balkan Mountains, they planned to rest in the city of Nish before they continued on the final leg of their journey. When they reached the city, they saw close-up the destruction caused by the Huns.

According to Priscus, the party smelled the city long before they saw it. The sickening odor of decayed corpses hung in the air. As he stood near a river that flowed past the city, Priscus wrote, "every place on the bank was full of the bones of those slain." The terrible sight served as reminder of Attila's ruthlessness.

Finally, after a journey of several months, the Romans reached Attila's court at Szeged on the Tisza River. After they set up their tents, the party was invited to a feast in Attila's palace. Priscus, like many people of

*By 449, Attila was feared throughout eastern Europe.*

the time, thought of "barbarians" as less than equals. This perception stemmed from the fact that those who spoke neither Greek nor Latin were considered uneducated and uncivilized foreigners. Thus, the Greek was surprised at the comfortable life of the Huns under Attila's rule. He wrote:

> *While sumptuous [costly] food, served in silver plates, had been prepared . . . for us, for Attila there was nothing but meat on a wooden platter. He showed himself temperate [modest] in . . . other ways, for gold and silver goblets [drinking mugs] were offered to the men at the feast, but his mug was of wood.*

Attila's dress also surprised Priscus, who was used to rulers who wore the finest clothing. Priscus observed: "His dress was plain, having care for nothing other than to be clean, nor was the sword by his side, nor the clasps of his boots . . . adorned [decorated] with gold or gems or anything of high price." Priscus, who knew nothing of the plot to kill Attila, was also impressed with the fierce loyalty that Attila's advisers and soldiers showed to him. Rather than fear the Hun leader, those closest to him admired him.

# Priscus Meets Attila's Wife

Much of what modern historians know about the daily life of Attila and the Huns comes from the writing of Priscus. It is believed that the Greek historian was born in Thrace early in the fifth century. Priscus is known to have written a history of the region that was eight volumes in length. Of those eight books, however, only a few fragments survive. One of them describes his visit in 449 as part of a Roman party with the Roman diplomat Maximinus to the court of Attila. At that time, the Huns were often described as cannibals and semihuman beasts. Priscus draws a picture of the Huns that is very different from other sources. In this short piece, he describes the royal living conditions of Attila's first wife.

*"The next day I entered the enclosure of Attila's palace, bearing gifts to his wife, whose name was Kreka.... Within the enclosure were numerous buildings, some of carved boards beautifully fitted together, others of straight [boards], fastened on round wooden blocks which rose to a moderate height from the ground. Attila's wife lived here, and, having been admitted by the barbarians at the door, I found her reclining on a soft couch. The floor of the room was covered with woolen mats for walking on. A number of servants stood round her, and maids sitting on the floor in front of her embroidered with colors linen cloths intended to be placed over [her] dress for ornament.*

Soon after the feast, Bigilas was brought before Attila when someone reported that the Roman possessed fifty pounds of gold. Priscus does not write who told Attila about the gold, but some historians suspect that it was Edika, who had misled the Romans from the start about his willingness to kill Attila. Edika is believed to have gone along with the Romans' plans, in order to reveal them for the dishonorable and cowardly people the Huns thought they were.

Bigilas was forced to his knees before the king of the Huns. Priscus writes that Attila roared at Bigilas, "No longer, you worthless beast, will . . . there be any excuse sufficient for you to escape punishment!"

The punishment surprised Priscus. Attila allowed Bigilas to live instead of sending him to a cruel death. He sent the Roman party back to Constantinople with a Hun guard, and Bigilas was forced to wear double the weight of the gold—100 pounds—around his neck in a bag for the entire journey. He was brought before Theodosius in that condition. It was Attila's way of showing his disrespect—by allowing Bigilas to live, Attila mocked Theodosius for sending a weakling on such an important mission.

## CHAPTER 4

# A TURN TO THE WEST

$\mathcal{D}$uring the years of the Huns' conquest in the East, a number of events had taken place in the Western Roman Empire. Among the most important occurred late in the fourth century when the rulers of the empire left Rome and moved the capital to the city of Ravenna. Rome had not only fallen into ruin, it had been decimated by the bubonic plague over the preceding two centuries.

Ravenna was located northeast of Rome, not far from the modern-day city of Bologna. It was protected from invaders by the sea to the

*The tomb of Galla Placida is one of the most famous structures built during the fifth century.*

ATTILA THE HUN

east and by dense swamps in the west. It was also located much closer than Rome to the Huns' homeland of Pannonia.

In the early fifth century, the most powerful person in Ravenna was a woman named Galla Placida. With her husband, the emperor Honorious, she had a son, Valentinian, and a daughter, Honoria. After the death of Honorious in 423, Galla Placida had her son declared the emperor—although he was only six years old. The child ruler left most of the governing decisions to his mother, and Galla Placida became the virtual ruler of the Western Roman Empire.

By 450, when Attila controlled much of eastern Europe, the Roman Empire was ruled by Theodosius II in Constantinople and by Valentinian in Ravenna, who was then in his early thirties. Honoria, Valentinian's younger sister, held the title of "augusta," or princess, but she was dissatisfied by her position in the court and had little respect for her brother.

Honoria, like her mother, sought the power of the throne. She attempted to take control by marrying a weak-willed noble named Eugenious. She plotted to murder her brother and make her husband the new emperor—which would put her in a position somewhat like the one her mother had once held.

61

# "THE BLACK DEATH"

Few, if any, diseases in human history have been more feared than the bubonic plague—known for centuries as "The Black Death." The disease killed one-third of the population of Europe in the 14th century, but that was not its first appearance in the West. The black death struck Rome with equally devastating results more than 1,000 years earlier.

Bubonic plague is a bacterial disease transmitted by fleas that feed on the blood of infected rodents. Those infected fleas in turn pass the bacteria into the blood of humans when they bite. Once it enters the bloodstream, the disease spreads quickly. Victims first become nauseated and run high fevers. As the disease progresses, it causes painful swelling in the lymph nodes of the groin, armpits, and neck. These nodes—called buboes—fill with blood and burst. This causes black spots under the skin that give the disease its common name.

The progress of the disease is very rapid once the first symptoms appear. A Roman author wrote that plague victims "had lunch with friends and dinner with their ancestors."

Scientists now believe that the plague was brought to Rome on ships that came into Roman ports from Asia. Infected rats left the ships and moved into settled areas to feed. In the years between 170 and 180 A.D., at least one-fourth of the population of the entire Roman Empire died from the disease. In 252 A.D., the plague began a fifteen-year devastation of Rome. During some years of that deadly epidemic, more than 5,000 people a day died in the city.

The black death remained one of the most feared diseases of ancient life for almost 2,000 years. The relation between flea bites and the plague was not discovered until the beginning of the twentieth century.

*Thousands of people a day died during the plagues that struck Roman cities.*

Valentinian, however, discovered the plot and had Eugenious killed. Rather than killing Honoria as well, he bowed to his dying mother's wishes and banished his sister to Constantinople to live with Theodosius II, a distant relative.

After more than 40 years on the throne, Theodosius still ruled in fear of an attack by the Huns. After Attila's discovery of the murder plot, the emperor had kept the Hun king away from Constantinople by increasing the tribute to more than 2,100 pounds of gold a year. Honoria realized soon after her arrival how much power Attila had over the Eastern Roman Empire. She saw an opportunity to gain power for herself in the East, and sent a messenger to Attila's court carrying her royal ring.

Attila knew right away what the ring represented: a proposal of marriage. He had never met Honoria, but this opportunity was too important to ignore. Despite the fact that he already had 18 wives, the Hun king now had a chance to gain control of an empire without fighting a single battle.

When word of Honoria's proposal reached Theodosius, the emperor was furious. The marriage would put Attila one step from the Roman throne he had held for so long and paid so much to keep.

Theodosius immediately sent the young woman back to Ravenna.

This action turned Attila's attention from the East to the West. When he learned that Honoria had returned to Ravenna, Attila sent a party of Huns to the capital of the Western Roman Empire. He sent word that he accepted Honoria's marriage proposal, and that the Hun custom called for a woman to offer a dowry—a marriage gift—to her desired husband. Attila said that for a dowry he wanted control of half of the Western Roman Empire.

Valentinian, who was seen by many as a weak emperor, decided that to keep his people's respect, he had to stand up to the fierce Hun king. He sent word back to Attila that under no circumstances would he agree to such a dowry. Attila greeted that decision by declaring war. He ordered his huge army to march against the Romans, although he knew that the war would be difficult because he would be facing Valentinian's most skilled general—Aetius, his own boyhood friend.

## "The Scourge of God"

Although he held the throne for just eight years, Attila's reputation has lasted for centuries. The reason for the Hun king's impact on history and legends, most historians

65

Attila moved his
enormous army quickly
across western Europe.

agree, is a result of his invasion of western Europe, and of his final battle with Aetius.

In 450, Attila left the main Hun settlement of Szeged, and moved west with an army that is believed to have been as large as 100,000 men. Usually, an army of that size would move slowly, but because the Roman system of roads was so extensive and well built, the army moved quickly west. They had soon traveled across the northern frontier of the empire and crossed the Rhine River. At that point, they invaded cities in the huge Roman province of Gaul, a region that encompassed the modern-day countries of France, Switzerland, and Belgium.

As he had during his campaign of 447, Attila hoped that his brutal conquest of the initial cities in his path would lead to easier conquests as he marched farther into Gaul. He devastated and depopulated the cities he conquered just as he had done in his campaign against Theodosius. This time, the damage was even worse because Gaul had more cities than the region around Constantinople.

Priests, who in those times were among the few people who could read and write, usually wrote the reports of cities attacked by Attila. Because the destruction was unlike any the priests had ever witnessed, many

The Roman Empire
450 A.D.

The empire at the
time of Attila the Hun

370 → Hun's invasion
route and year

of their reports claimed that the Huns attacked to punish the people of a certain city for their sins.

In other words, Attila was not seen as a military leader. He was viewed more as a punishment—or "scourge"—of God. As the Huns advanced, religious writers in city after city described the invasions in terms such as these from Gregory of Tours: "The Huns... gave the city to the flames and slew (killed) the people with the edge of the sword, and did to death the priests of the Lord before Holy altars."

For the last weeks of 450 and into early 451, Attila's army made its way west across France, and destroyed every city in its path until it reached Paris, a small walled city on an island in the Seine River. Among the people in Paris was a teenage nun named Genevieve. When word came that the Huns were near the city, panic spread. Genevieve, however, stood up in a church where frightened Parisians had gone to pray. She told the audience that she would go out to meet Attila with a group of young girls and refuse to allow his army to attack. The legendary meeting between the young woman and the fierce Hun ended when Attila ordered his army to turn away from Paris and march south.

The story of Genevieve's bravery not only spread during the months of Attila's campaign, it was passed

*Genevieve became the patron saint of Paris as a result of her bravery against Attila and his army.*

down through the centuries by those who followed the Christian faith. She was named a saint in the Catholic faith, and today is the patron saint of Paris.

## The Resistance Stiffens

Attila may have decided to march south from Paris because larger cities such as Orleans and Tours offered greater riches. Another key reason for turning south may have been to capture Toulouse, a city in what is today southern France. That city was the capital of the Visigoth empire. The Visigoths, led by their king, Theodoric, were a powerful fighting force, and had already taken control of a large region of Gaul from the Romans. The Visigoths held an especially bitter hatred toward the Huns—under Ruga, the Huns had forced the Visigoths out of Pannonia at the end of the fourth century. Attila knew that he had to defeat Theodoric to gain control of the Western Roman Empire.

Despite previous battles with Roman legions, by 451, the Visigoths under Theodoric had built good relations with the Romans. Relations were so good, in fact, that Roman forces under Aetius had crossed the Alps from Italy and joined Theodoric's troops in response to Attila's advance. This meant that, for the first time, Attila's army was opposed by a force that was equal to his own in size.

In late spring 451, Attila's army reached the large walled city of Orleans. The troops launched an attack with battering rams in an effort to break down the city's walls. The Huns met unexpected resistance—soldiers stationed on the walls showered the attackers with arrows, stones, and boiling oil. Attila had no way of knowing that those troops were part of a large force that Aetius had sent from Toulouse to slow the Huns' advance.

Despite the fierce resistance, Attila's forces continued to batter the walls. They finally stopped when scouts returned to the Hun encampment with word that a huge force was advancing toward them from the south—a force made of the combined armies of Theodoric and Aetius.

## The Battle of Châlons

After he halted his attack on Orleans, Attila had to decide on the best location for a battle against the forces of Theodoric and Aetius. He had to find an area where nearly 100,000 soldiers could battle on foot, an area that could be defended if his men were overrun by the enemy. He was forced to set up defensive positions; to do this, he formed war wagons into walls and dug trenches.

Although the location of the actual battlefield has never been found, ancient records refer to the encounter as the Battle of Châlons or the Battle of the

Catalaunian Fields—flat areas outside of the city of Châlons. The opposing forces gathered there in late June 451. Before he sent his men into battle, Attila, seated on his horse, addressed them. Attila knew that his men needed little encouragement to fight. A Roman historian, Jordanes, described the Hun king's speech to his immense force of Huns and other eastern Europeans. "Here you stand after conquering mighty nations and subduing the world," he said. "It is foolish for me to goad (encourage) you with words, as though you were men who had not been proved in action.... For what is war but your usual custom?... It is a right of nature to glut the soul with vengeance."

Attila went on to insult the forces that opposed them. He seemed to forget for a moment that his own army was made up of men from various tribes: "Despise this union of discordant [differing] races. To defend oneself by alliance is proof of cowardice. See, even before our attack they are smitten [overcome] with terror.... Let your courage rise and your own fury burst forth."

Finally, Attila spoke of his great pride as a Hun and his love of battle and bloodshed. He finished his speech, then picked up his spear and galloped toward the enemy lines. The battle was under way.

Attila's archers launched a thick cloud of arrows as the enemy began its charge. The Hun cavalry, led by the fierce king, galloped to the front of the charge. Soon, the opposing lines of soldiers clashed, and long hours of hand-to-hand combat began.

Jordanes described the fighting as "fierce, confused, monstrous, and unrelenting." Blood flowed into a creek in the battlefield and turned it into a "raging current." Wounded men on both sides, driven mad by thirst, crawled to the stream and "drank water mingled with gore (blood)."

In the center of the conflict, Theodoric bravely rode among his Visigoths, and cheered them on. Suddenly, he was thrown from his horse and killed. The confusion that followed the Visigoth ruler's death allowed some of Attila's men to break through the center of the opposing line. That advantage faded quickly, however, when Aetius's fast-moving Romans broke through Attila's right flank and threatened to attack from the rear.

For the first time as a commander on a battlefield, Attila had to pull back his forces to prevent them from being surrounded. Attila immediately ordered a huge fire to be built behind his lines. He swore that if the Romans overran his defenses, he would throw himself into the fire rather than be captured.

*After Theodoric was killed, his son, Thorismund, took command of the Visigoth forces.*

As the sun sank over the Catalaunian fields, the Hun army withdrew to their wagons and trenches. Never before had Attila retreated from a battlefield. The Hun army remained behind its defenses, while the opposing forces removed their dead from the battlefield. The dead included the Visigoth king, Theodoric, whose place in command was taken by his son, Thorismund.

As they retreated across Gaul, the Huns carved a path of terror, destruction, and death.

Attila's main opponent, Aetius, immediately ordered his men to surround the Huns and place them under siege. Aetius knew that if the Huns could not move, they and their animals would soon run out of food and water.

Had Theodoric survived the battle, Aetius's planned siege might have worked. As it turned out, however, Thorismund had no intention of spending weeks or even months waiting to starve the Huns into surrender. As the new ruler of the Visigoths, he was eager to return to Toulouse and officially take the throne before others staked their claim to the crown. Soon after they cleared the battlefield of their dead, the Visigoths departed. This left Aetius no choice but to withdraw his troops from their positions.

The withdrawal caught Attila completely by surprise. He suspected a trick, so he kept his forces in their position long after Aetius had left. Finally, he too left the bloody fields. Attila's losses had been so great that he felt he could not continue toward Toulouse. Thus, the Huns' path of destruction through France ended, and they traveled the long road back to Pannonia.

There were, of course, other cities on the return home. The Huns destroyed them with a terrible fury— not to build their reputation but to avenge their failure at Châlons. One historian described the horror unleashed by the Huns' returning army: "They massacred their hostages as well as their captives, two hundred maidens were tortured with . . unrelenting rage. Their bodies were torn asunder [apart] by wild horses . . or crushed under the weight of rolling wagons." Even in defeat, the Huns left an unforgettable image in the minds of Romans and other people throughout Europe.

## CHAPTER 5

# THE INVASION OF ITALY

Upon his return to the main settlement at Szeged, Attila resumed his demands for tribute from the Eastern Roman emperor at Constantinople. By that time, the emperor Theodosius was dead, and the new ruler, Marcian, had received word of the outcome at Châlons. He knew that Attila's army had been seriously weakened, and that his reputation had been damaged. He believed that the Hun king was in no position to back up his threats, and he refused to pay tribute to Attila.

Once, the simple threat of a Hun attack had been enough to draw payments of gold from frightened rulers. Now emperors dared Attila to attack. The Hun kingdom, which relied mainly on tribute to keep its economy strong, was in a difficult situation. The army was not powerful enough to march against Constantinople. It had already taken all the treasure it could from Gaul and western Europe. That left only one region to attack—Italy and its heart, the once great city of Rome.

Early in the spring of 452, Attila and his army set out for the Italian peninsula. Although Rome was no longer the capital of the empire, it was still the most famous city in the western world. Attila believed that conquering Rome might rebuild his power and his reputation.

The Hun army left Pannonia and crossed the Alps into northeastern Italy near the border of the modern country of Slovenia. Their first target was the walled city of Aquileia. At the time, it was an important city in Italy because it was located on a narrow passage into Italy and was intended to keep non-Roman armies from invading. Attila decided to lay siege to Aquileia and starve the city into surrender, instead of attacking and losing troops he might need later in the campaign.

81

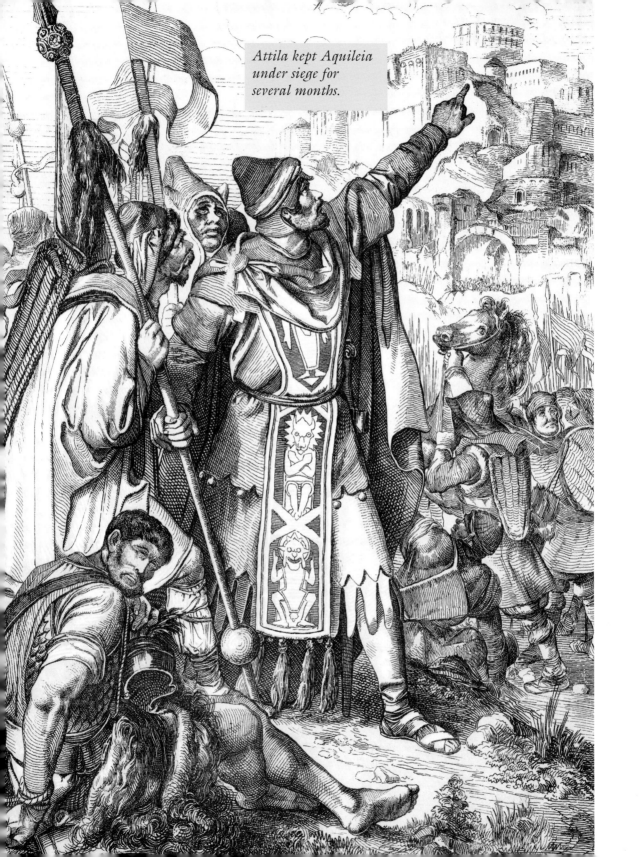

*Attila kept Aquileia under siege for several months.*

The people of the city held out against the Huns for three months. The siege of Aquileia did not cost the Huns any lives. It did, however, cost them valuable time. During the siege, summer had come, and if winter set in before the Huns reached Rome, the cold weather would reduce the amount of food that could be taken from the countryside.

Finally, just as Attila was about to withdraw his army from the siege, part of the city wall collapsed. Aquileia was at the mercy of the Huns, who destroyed it and all its inhabitants with a ruthless attack. The city was left in ruins and never rebuilt.

## The March on Rome

As word of the destruction of Aquileia spread, however, other cities in the path of the Huns chose not to resist the army's advance. As the army moved west, then turned south, city after city fell. Attila's men laid waste to each place after they took every possible item of value.

As they marched southward, the Hun army did not attack the city of Ravenna, the capital of the Western Roman Empire. Historians believe that Attila avoided the city because the forces that protected it were under the command of Aetius. In Ravenna, Aetius wanted to leave the city to meet Attila on the battlefield once again, but the emperor, Valentinian, would not allow Aetius to leave his city unprotected. As the Huns destroyed historic Roman cities such as Milan, Verona, and Vicenza, Aetius insisted that he be allowed to face Attila. Valentinian continued to refuse, and the feelings between the two powerful men grew extremely bitter.

As the summer came to an end, Attila's force reached the city of Mediolanum in central Italy. The city had briefly served as the Roman capital a century earlier. Attila took control of the city's royal palace, and sat on the throne that had held the most powerful rulers in the world. The walls of the throne room were decorated with paintings of several emperors who had ruled from the city. Attila ordered an artist from the city to add his portrait to the wall—a portrait that showed him seated on a throne as he looked down on past emperors.

Then, because he wanted to reach Rome before the weather turned cold, Attila ordered his army to continue the march south. The huge force eventually reached the Mincio River. There, one of the most famous encounters in history took place.

## A Legendary Meeting

Although Rome was no longer the capital of the Western Roman Empire, it was a city of great importance in 452 because it was the center of the Christian religion. The leader of the faith, the pope, ruled the city that had once been the capital of the greatest empire on Earth. Pope Leo I, known as "Leo the Great," led the Christians from 430 until 460.

When word reached Rome that Attila's forces were approaching, Leo decided to meet the Hun leader outside of the city. As the young nun Genevieve had done outside of Paris, Leo planned to ask Attila to spare the city. Accompanied by two Roman senators, Leo met Attila on the banks of the Mincio River. What happened between the men has become part of a legend of the early Christian church, and has been the subject of many paintings by famous artists.

According to the legend, Attila was lying on a couch in his tent when Leo arrived. Because he was not a Christian—and had been especially brutal to Christians—Attila did not show Leo the respect that other Christian rulers did. At first, Attila refused Leo's appeal to turn back from his goal of conquering Rome. Suddenly, however, Attila saw a vision of St. Peter and St. Paul, two of the founders of the Christian faith, standing on either side of the pope. The saints warned Attila that he would die instantly if he did not obey Leo's request. The vision was so frightening, legend

85

*Pope Leo I met Attila on the banks of the Mincio River.*

says, that Attila ordered his army to turn away and return to Pannonia.

The story of the meeting between Leo and Attila was widely accepted for centuries. Several famous paintings and other works of art were created to show the event. Some historians, however, offer different reasons for Attila's decision to end his conquest of Italy.

One key reason for the withdrawal may have been disease. Records show that malaria had struck down a huge number of the Hun soldiers. The army may well have been too weakened to conquer a huge city such as Rome, some historians say.

Historical records also show that there had been a drought in Italy for a year before Attila invaded. As a result, there was a shortage of food for the invading army and little grass for the Hun horses. The campaign may have ended because Attila feared his force would face starvation.

Finally, the three-month delay at the siege of Aquileia meant there was less time for Attila to conquer Rome before winter arrived. He had to decide whether to risk having his army caught in cold weather with little food or return to the safety of his homeland for the winter. Attila had conquered several large cities and taken great wealth for his treasury. He may have decided that he

# THE FAMOUS MEETING

The story of the meeting between Pope Leo I and Attila the Hun was told and retold throughout the Middle Ages. One anonymous writer described the encounter this way:

*Attila...was utterly cruel in inflicting torture, greedy in plundering, insolent in abuse....He destroyed Aquileia from the foundations,...laid waste many other towns, and was rushing down upon Rome.*

*Then Leo...ready of his own will to give himself entirely for the defense of his flock, went forth to meet the tyrant....He met Attila, it is said, in the neighborhood of the Mincio River, and he spoke to the grim monarch, saying "O Attila, thou king of kings, thou couldst have no greater glory than to see...at thy feet this peo-ple before whom once all peoples and kings lay. Thou hast subdued, O Attila, the...lands... granted to the Romans. Now we pray that thou, who hast conquered others, shouldst conquer thyself. The people have felt thy scourge; now...they would feel thy mercy."*

*As Leo said these things Attila stood...silent, as if thinking deeply. And lo, suddenly there were seen the apostles Peter and Paul, clad like bishops, standing by Leo, the one on the right hand, the other on the left. They held swords stretched out over his head, and threatened Attila with death if he did not obey the pope's command. Wherefore Attila,...by Leo's intercession, straightway promised a lasting peace and withdrew beyond the Danube.*

The meeting of Pope Leo I and Attila was the subject of a number of paintings during the Middle Ages.

could return to conquer Rome and make a prisoner of the pope the following year.

Whatever the reason for his decision, Attila ordered his army to begin the long journey home. By the end of 452, Attila was back in his palace in Szeged to await the end of winter. The Hun king was not idle during the cold weather. He negotiated ransoms with the leaders of conquered cities for the return of wealthy citizens he had captured during his campaign into Italy. In this way, Attila's wealth grew while he remained at peace.

## CHAPTER 6

# THE END OF EMPIRES

Although he left Italy without conquering Rome, Attila still controlled an enormous area of land and possessed great wealth. The Huns had destroyed more than 100 cities, stolen countless treasures, and killed hundreds of thousands of people across Europe. After only eight years as king, Attila had become one of the most powerful men in the world. During the winter of 453, he sent messengers to Marcian in Constantinople, again with a demand that Marcian pay the same gold tribute that Theodosius had paid. Attila also demanded control over lands that Theodosius had once promised the Huns.

Marcian refused the Hun king once more. In response, Attila planned to invade the Eastern Roman Empire in the spring of 453.

At some time during that winter, Attila decided to take another wife. Her name was Idilco, and she was said to be young and beautiful. Little else is known about her life or how she met Attila, who was then about 47 years old and already had eighteen wives and more than fifty children.

Attila's wedding to Idilco became a wild celebration at his palace in Szeged. There was a feast and endless amounts of wine for the guests. Many toasts were offered to the couple, and songs that praised the bravery of Attila were sung hour after hour.

Throughout his life, Attila had been moderate in his eating and drinking habits. On that night, however, he stayed up late and drank a great deal of wine. He was at the height of his powers and enjoyed the praise. He went to bed as dawn broke, and told his servants that he intended to sleep through most of the day.

The historian Jordanes described the events that followed: "On the following day . . . the royal attendants suspected some ill and, after a great uproar, broke in the doors. There they found . . . Attila . . . in an effusion [pool] of blood, without any wound."

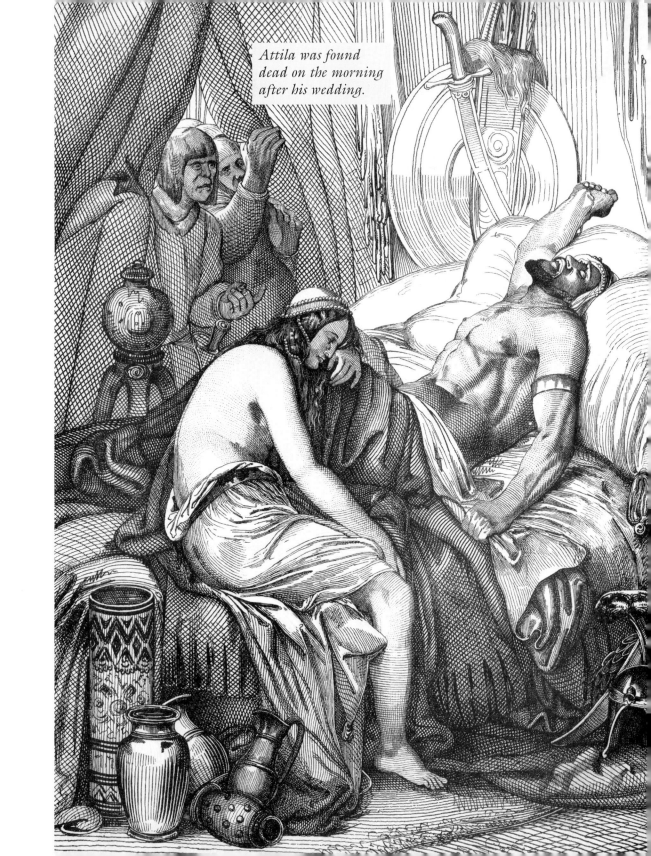

Attila was found dead on the morning after his wedding.

Attendants who examined the king discovered that a blood vessel in Attila's nose had burst while he was in a deep, drunken sleep. He had drowned in his own blood. The king of the Huns, one of the most ferocious leaders in history, had died from a bloody nose.

Attila had faced death in battle countless times, and most Huns considered him immortal. Thus his death came as an enormous shock to them. Suddenly, one of the great empires in history was left without the leader under whose guidance the Huns had become the most feared warriors in the world.

In accordance with Hun custom, Attila's body was laid under a silk canopy in the middle of a large field. The most skilled horsemen of the tribe galloped wildly around the body of the fallen king in order to please him before his journey to the next world. Men and women who had sung songs at his wedding a few days earlier now sang songs that praised Attila as the greatest of all Hun kings—the man who brought Roman emperors to their knees, conquered their cities, and took enormous wealth from the Roman Empire.

The warriors who had served longest at Attila's side cut off their hair and slashed their faces with knives. This was the Hun way to honor a fallen king. The burial soon followed—an event reported by Jordanes years later:

*In the secrecy of night they buried his body. . . . They bound his coffin first with gold, second with silver, and third with . . . iron. They also added arms won in . . . battle . . . of rare worth, sparkling with gems and ornaments of all sorts.*

Jordanes then described one final act of Hun brutality. "That so great riches might be kept from human curiosity they slew [killed] those appointed to do the work [burial], a dreadful reward for their labor. Thus sudden death was the lot of those who buried him as well as of him who was buried."

The actual burial site of Attila is one of history's great mysteries. Some archeologists believe that the coffin is buried in western Hungary somewhere between the Tisza and Danube Rivers—an area of more than 13,000 square miles. Among Hungarians, the legend has been passed down that Attila was buried at the bottom of either the Tisza or Danube Rivers to prevent grave robbers from taking the treasure buried with the king.

## The Huns After Attila

Soon after the death of Attila, his oldest son, Ellak, became king. He was supported by his father's closest military advisers and may have planned to continue as complete ruler, like Attila, but this arrangement was not to be.

Ellak had two younger brothers who also wanted a share of the power handed down from Attila. One brother was named Dengzik. The other was Ernak, who was widely known to have been his father's favorite son. The two younger brothers wanted the Hun kingdom divided in the way it had been when Attila and Bleda shared power. Instead of territory, however, Ellak gave his brothers control over some of the peoples that the Huns had conquered. This proved to be a decision that weakened the Hun empire.

By this point, many of the conquered peoples had recovered from the devastation that the Huns had wrought on them years earlier. Many soldiers in Attila's army, in fact, had been drawn from conquered peoples. Now, back in their homelands, with the formerly united rule of the Huns divided between three brothers, there was an opportunity to turn the tables on the Huns.

Within a year after Attila's death, fighting broke out between the various peoples who supported the different brothers. Other, more powerful, tribes saw an opportunity to attack the Huns while the brothers fought among themselves. In 455, a huge army made up of barbarian tribes from the modern countries of

Germany, Italy, and Iran met the Huns on the banks of a river called the Nedao. The Huns were defeated, and Ellak was killed. The majority of the Hun Empire fell under the control of a people known as the Gepids, who had once served as farmers and laborers under the Huns.

The two younger brothers did not succeed either. In 466, Dengzik was defeated and killed in a battle against the army of the Eastern Roman Empire. His skull was brought to Constantinople and put on public display as revenge for the destruction his father had caused.

Ernak was a more cautious leader. Aware that he could not raise an army large enough to defeat the combined forces of the Eastern Roman Empire as his father had, he asked to be allowed to become a Roman citizen. In addition, he asked for a grant of land near the mouth of the Danube River in modern Romania. There he established a small homeland for the Hun people, and they faded from the world stage.

## Attila's Moment in History

Within a year after Attila's death, the man who had stopped his advance across Gaul also met his end. Aetius had rebuilt the Roman army into a respectable fighting force, and other Romans, especially those not in the military, were jealous of his power. These men, senators and wealthy merchants, spread a rumor that Aetius planned to assassinate the emperor, Valentinian, and take the throne for himself. Valentinian, however, was determined to hold on to power and killed an unarmed Aetius during a meeting in the emperor's chambers.

That murder indirectly helped bring a final end to the Roman Empire in the West. Without a strong commander, the Roman army was again weakened. Barbarians attacked throughout the empire at will. In 476, a little more than 20 years after Attila's death, Emperor Romulus Augustus—the son of Orestes, Attila's closest adviser—was forced from the throne. Romulus is considered the last emperor of the Western Roman Empire.

In the long history of Rome and Europe, eight years is an extremely short length of time. Yet, for Attila, eight years was enough to make his name one of the most notorious in world history. Historians have long argued over the reason for Attila's fame. He was not the most successful conqueror of his time—most of the Hun Empire had been formed by his uncle, father, and brother. He did not conquer Rome. And while he did bring great wealth into the Hun kingdom, that kingdom did not survive his death.

Attila, however, was feared more than any other leader of his time. Some historians believe this is because he was Asian. His religious beliefs were derived from his Hunnish roots and were viewed as superstitions by Roman Christians. Other so-called barbarian tribes became Roman citizens and converted to Christianity at some point during their history. Attila and the Huns continued to sacrifice animals to various gods, a practice that was considered sacrilegious by that time.

In his time, the Hun ruler was considered a barbarian for his religious practices and his inability to speak Latin or Greek. His cruel and destructive conquests made him the person most associated with the modern definition of a barbarian—a ruthless destroyer. Attila's mere presence commanded fear in everyone of his day, from Roman citizens to lowly peasants.

Attila was not the beloved leader of his people, either. Although he is credited as the only ruler of the Huns who was able to unite a nomadic people under a single ruler, he did so in an underhanded way by having his older brother murdered.

The only known description of him, by Priscus, presents Attila as a menacing presence. Had he not died suddenly, historians believe, there is a strong possibility

*Although Attila ruled for only eight years, his legend has lasted centuries. This play, from the early twentieth century, told the story of Idilco and Attila.*

ATTILA THE HUN

that Attila would once again have attacked and perhaps overthrown the Eastern Roman Empire at Constantinople.

Perhaps the best evidence of the Hun king's villainy is simply that his image and reputation continued to grow after his death and after his people had faded from history. Unlike the reputations of other successful barbarian kings—Alaric, Theodoric, and others—Attila's legend has lasted for centuries.

In the end, Jordanes best sums up Attila, the warrior and king, with these words: "He was a man born into the world to shake the nations, the scourge of all lands, who in some way terrified all mankind by the dreadful rumors noised abroad concerning him. He was haughty in his walk, rolling his eyes here and there, so that the power of his proud spirit appeared in the movement of his body. He was indeed a lover of war, yet restrained in action, mighty in counsel, gracious to supplicants and lenient to those who were once received into his protection."

# CHRONOLOGY

The 200 years between 300 and 500 A.D. were some of the most horrifying times in European history. Empires fell, countless deaths occurred, and many in the West believed that the world was coming to an end. Here is a timeline of two centuries of turmoil.

**306–337**    Constantine rules the Roman Empire.

**312**    Constantine converts to Christianity.

**330**    Constantinople becomes the capital of Constantine's empire.

**376**    Visigoths are forced from Pannonia by the Huns.

**395**    The Roman Empire is officially divided into Eastern and Western Empires.

**c. 406**    Attila is born.

**408**    Theodosius II becomes emperor of the Eastern Roman Empire at age seven.

**422**    King Ruga and the Huns defeat the armies of Theodosius II at Thrace. The emperor agrees to yearly tribute of 350 pounds of gold.

**425**    Valentinian III becomes emperor of Western Roman Empire.

**434**    Ruga dies; Bleda and Attila share the rule of the Huns.

| 435 | Bleda and Attila agree to the Treaty of Margus with Theodosius II. Tribute increases to 700 pounds of gold. |
| 437–440 | Bleda and Attila conquer lands in the Alps and Rhine River region. |
| 444 | Bleda dies under mysterious circumstances. |
| 445 | Attila becomes sole ruler of the Huns. |
| 447 | Attila, in his first military campaign, conquers more than 70 cities in the Balkan Peninsula and Greece. Disease among his troops prevents an assault on Constantinople. |
| 449 | Court of Theodosius plots to assassinate Attila. The plot is uncovered, and Attila forces the Roman tribute to grow to 2,100 pounds of gold per year. |
| 450 | Honoria sends a marriage proposal to Attila. He demands half of the Western Roman Empire as a dowry. Emperor Valentinian III refuses, and Attila declares war. |
| 450–451 | Attila conquers much of Gaul, and destroys cities in modern-day Austria, Germany, Belgium, and France. |
| 451 | Battle of Châlons. Attila is defeated by combined forces of Aetius and Theodoric. |
| 452 | Attila invades and conquers much of northern Italy. As he advances on Rome, he meets Pope Leo I at the Mincio River and turns back. |

| 453 | Attila dies in his sleep. His sons, Ellak, Dungzik, and Ernak take control of the Hun empire. |
|---|---|
| 454 | Valentinian III kills Aetius. |
| 455 | Ellak is defeated by the Gepids and barbarian forces. |
| 466 | Dundzik is defeated by forces of the Eastern Roman Empire. |
| 469 | Ernak becomes a Roman citizen and rules a Hun homeland near the mouth of the Danube River. |
| 476 | Western Roman Empire falls. |

ATTILA THE HUN

# GLOSSARY

**alliance**  An association of nations or peoples.

**barbarians**  People from outside Roman borders.

**cavalry**  Soldiers mounted on horseback.

**dowry**  Money, goods, or land offered for marriage.

**emperor**  Supreme ruler of an empire.

**drought**  Prolonged period without precipitation.

**malaria**  Blood disease carried by mosquitoes.

**migrate**  To move from one country or region to another.

**nomads**  People who have no established homeland.

**siege**  A military blockade of a city or fortified position.

**steppes**  Grasslands in central Asia.

**tribute**  A payment to acknowledge submission to a conqueror.

# Source Notes

## Introduction

Page 5: "short of stature..." by Deither Etzel,
*I'm a Barbarian* web site
http://art1.candor.com/barbarian/attila.htm#Hun

Page 7: "Seek swift victory..." Howarth, Patrick. *Attila King of the Huns.* New York, Carrol & Graf 2001
p. 110–111.

## Chapter 1

Page 15: "In village, villa, field..." Professor Gerhard Rempel website *Tribal Migrations*
http://mars.acnet.wnec.edu/~grempel/courses/wc1/lectures/15tribes.html

Page 16: "large heads...protruding eyes..." Howarth, Patrick. *Attila King of the Huns.* New York, Carrol & Graf 2001 p. 19.

Page 25: "When attacked they sometimes engage in regular battle..." Arthur Ferrill *Attila the Hun*
http://history.cc.ukans.edu/carrie/texts/ferrill1.art

Page 27: "The nation of Huns..." Ibid.

## Chapter 2

Page 42: It is the wholesome life..." Howarth, Patrick. *Attila King of the Huns.* New York, Carrol & Graf 2001 p. 76.

## Chapter 3

Page 49: "There were so many murders..." Arthur Ferrill *Attila the Hun*
http://history.cc.ukans.edu/carrie/texts/ferrill1.art

Page 54: "every place on the bank..." Howarth, Patrick. *Attila King of the Huns*. New York, Carrol & Graf 2001 p. 69.

Page 56: "While sumptuous food..." Howarth, Patrick. *Attila King of the Huns*. New York, Carrol & Graf 2001 p. 73.

Page 57: "The next day I entered..." Howarth, Patrick. *Attila King of the Huns*. New York, Carrol & Graf 2001 p. 77.

Page 58: "No longer you worthless beast..." Ibid. p 76

## Chapter 4

Page 69: The Huns...gave the city to flames..." Howarth. p 99.

Page 73: "Here you stand..." Howarth. p. 109.

Page 74: "fierce, confused, monstrous..." Howarth p. 113.

Page 79: "They massacred their hostages..." Howarth p. 119.

## Chapter 5

Page 88: "Attila was utterly cruel..." Howarth p. 133.

## Chapter 6

Page 92: "On the following day..." Howarth p. 138.

Page 95: "In the secrecy..." Howarth p. 139.

Page 101: "He was a man..." Howarth p. 16.

# FOR FURTHER READING

Howarth, Patrick. *Attila: King of the Huns. New York:* Carrol and Graf, 2001.

Nicolle, David. *Attila and the Nomad Hordes.* Oxford, U.K.: Osprey, 1997.

Nicolle, David. *Attila the Hun.* Oxford, U.K.: Osprey, 2001.

# WEBSITES

**Attila the Hun and the Barbarians**
*http://art1.candor.com/barbarian/*
Detailed site with information about Attila and other peoples of the time.

**Attila the Hun and the Battle of Châlons**
*http://www.rm-f.net/~zdv/attila.html*
Site with detailed information about the famous battle.

**Central Asian Nomads**
*http://members.tripod.com/great-bulgaria/*
*Central-Asian-Nomads-Unite/origins.html*
Good history of the origin of the Hun and other peoples of central Asia.

**The Roman Empire**
*http://www.roman-empire.net/*
Extremely detailed site about the history of the Roman Empire.

# INDEX